# LET THERE BE PEACE



Total Rejection of War as a Means of Resolving Conflict

*Robert A. Brooks*

# Table of Contents

# CHAPTER 1: INTRODUCTION

In a world filled with turmoil and suffering, a quaint village

emerged, encircled by lush hills and sparkling rivers. This village, called Harmony's Haven, was a peaceful and calm place, unaffected by the noise of war and fighting that happened nearby.

Jane, a young girl at the center of Harmony's Haven, wanted peace deeply. She had bright and hopeful eyes. She had lovely golden hair that looked like a waterfall, and her blue eyes were filled with innocence. She strongly believed that there must be a better way to solve problems instead of using violence and causing damage.

Little Jane loved hearing stories about history, like battles and the sad things that happen because of war, that stuck with people who were there. As she heard the older people talk about these sad truths, a strong feeling of determination and hope grew inside her. It made her want to question and fight against the idea that war is something humans always have to experience.

Jane was very determined to bring peace, so she decided to look into the history books to find people who had chosen not to fight in order to solve their problems. She eagerly read every book and scroll she could find. In doing so, she discovered stories about amazing people and groups who had chosen different ways to achieve peace.

Jane went on a journey outside Harmony's Haven because she had learned new things. She traveled through difficult terrains, faced tough challenges, and came across different cultures and beliefs on her journey. As more and more people learned about Jane's journey, people from different backgrounds and lifestyles found her determination to be very inspiring. The warriors, carrying heavy swords and armor, felt hopeful about a future where there would be no more fighting. Leaders and diplomats are having thoughtful discussions. They are thinking about a world where talking and understanding can replace fighting in battles.

Jane led a growing movement of people who didn't believe in war as a way to solve conflicts. They wanted a world where people talked and cared about each other, where people chose to understand each other instead of being mean.

This book is titled "Let There Be Peace. This story follows Jane and the people she has inspired on an exciting journey. In the next few pages, we will learn about both the accomplishments and difficulties of the movement. We will also hear heartwarming stories of individuals who found solace in peace, and see the determined efforts to create a peaceful world.

Come join Jane as she writes about her important goal, a goal that is still important today. She wants us all to think about whether war is necessary and to appreciate the great impact peace can have. This story called "Let There Be Peace" invites all of us to create a better future where there is no more war and everyone works together in harmony. It teaches us that peace is not just important, but necessary.

## BACKGROUND OF THE DESIRE FOR PEACE AND THE AVERSION TO WAR

The want for peace and the abhorrence of war has profound roots in human history and are formed by different variables. Here are a few key angles to consider when examining the foundation of this crave:

**1. Humanity:** At our center, people for the most part long for security, steadiness, and agreement. The fear, annihilation, and enduring caused by war are contradictory to these principal human desires. As social creatures, we have advanced to esteem participation, sympathy, and tranquil determination of clashes.

**2. Historic Period:** History serves as a strong update of the obliterating results of war. The repulsions of major clashes such as World Wars I and II, the Cold War, and different territorial clashes have cleared out permanent marks on social orders, economies, and endless lives. These collective encounters have affected a broad crave to maintain a strategic distance from rehashing such disastrous occasions.

**3. Advancement and advance:** Countries recognize that delayed clashes hinder advance and improvement. War redirects assets from foundation, instruction, healthcare, and other vital segments. The want for peace stems from the understanding that soundness and participation are crucial for financial development, social well-being, and generally human headway.

**4. Universal participation:** The rise of globalization has connected the world more closely, cultivating interdependencies among countries. Nations presently have motivations to look for quiet resolutions since clashes can have far-reaching results past their borders. As a result, discretion, transaction, and multilateral educate have picked up unmistakable quality as implies to settle debate and keep up peace.

**5. Helpful contemplations:** The compassionate toll of war is colossal, with civilians frequently bearing the brunt. The enduring, relocation, and misfortune of life experienced amid clashes bring out kindness and a ethical commitment to anticipate war. Developments pushing for human rights, pacifism, demobilization, and struggle determination have developed to maintain the esteem of human life and advance quiet choices.

**6. Lawful systems:** Worldwide law, counting the Joined together Countries Constitution, the Geneva Traditions, and other settlements, has been set up to direct and restrain the utilize of constrain between countries. These lawful systems advance tranquil debate determination, dishearten hostility, and give a premise for equity and responsibility.

**7. Social and devout impacts:** Numerous societies and religions advance values of peace, absolution, and non-violence. Concepts such as ahimsa (non-violence) in Hinduism, the Christian tenet of "fair war," or the lessons of peace in Buddhism embody the impact of otherworldly and moral convictions in cultivating a want for peace.

**8. Communication and innovation:** Progresses in communication innovation have made it less demanding for individuals around the world to put through and get it one another. Expanded worldwide interconnecting has encouraged exchange, sympathy, and the sharing of thoughts, driving to more noteworthy acknowledgment and appreciation of assorted viewpoints, cultivating peace-building endeavors.

By and large, the want for peace and abhorrence to war are profoundly imbued in human awareness and are molded by authentic encounters, social impacts, contemplations of advance, and a developing acknowledgment of our shared duties in an interconnected world.

# IMPORTANCE OF ADVOCATING FOR PEACE AND UNDERSTANDING ITS BENEFITS

Supporting peace is of foremost significance in today's world. It goes past the nonattendance of struggle and includes cultivating shared understanding, regard, and participation among people, communities, and countries. Understanding the benefits that come with peace is significant to advance such promotion. Here could be a nitty gritty diagram of the significance of supporting for peace and its benefits:

## 1. Lessening of savagery and human enduring:

a. Tranquil social orders encounter lower rates of viciousness, wrongdoing, and strife, driving to a more secure environment for people to flourish and succeed.

b. Supporting for peace advances the security of human rights, decreasing the enduring caused by war, uprooting, and mistreatment.

## 2. Socio-economic improvement:

a. Quiet countries advantage from expanded soundness, empowering more noteworthy financial development, speculation, and exchange.

b. Pushing for peace cultivates an environment conducive to the improvement of foundation, instruction, healthcare, and destitution decrease.

## 3. Conservation of vote-based system and run the show of law:

a. Peace permits for the conservation of equitable values, permitting citizens to take part effectively in decision-making.

b. Pushing for peace incorporates pushing for the run the show of law and the foundation of fair and reasonable lawful frameworks.

**4. Upgrading social cohesion and concordance:**

a. Tranquil social orders advance inclusivity, differing qualities, and social agreement by empowering discourse and understanding among diverse societies, religions, and ethnicities.

b. Pushing for peace makes a difference construct bridge and address deep-rooted societal divisions, cultivating social cohesion and a sense of having a place for all individuals of society.

**5. Natural supportability:**

a. Peace plays a imperative part in securing the environment as clashes regularly lead to natural debasement and ruin maintainability endeavors.

b. Pushing for peace includes advancing maintainable hones, tending to climate alter, and guaranteeing the conservation of normal assets for future eras.

## 6. Worldwide participation and discretion:

a. Peace permits for the foundation of worldwide collusions, participation, and strategy for settling clashes, tending to worldwide challenges, and advancing shared thriving.

b. Pushing for peace contributes to making a worldwide culture of exchange, arrangement, and serene determination of debate.

## 7. Individual well-being and mental wellbeing:

a. Tranquil situations emphatically affect individuals' mental wellbeing and by and large well-being, decreasing stretch, uneasiness, and injury.

b. Supporting for peace incorporates advancing mental wellbeing, well-being, and the arrangement of bolster frameworks for those influenced by viciousness and strife.

In rundown, pushing for peace is basic due to its wide-ranging benefits. These benefits incorporate the decrease of viciousness and human enduring, socio-economic advancement, conservation of vote-based system and run the show of law, upgrading social cohesion and concordance, natural supportability, worldwide participation and discretion, and individual well-being. Understanding these benefits fortifies the noteworthiness of pushing for peace, making it a essential interest for people, communities, and countries.

# CHAPTER 2: THE COSTS OF WAR

## THE DEVASTATING IMPACT OF WAR ON INDIVIDUALS, FAMILTIES AND SOCIETIES AT LARGE

War, whether it happens between countries or within a country, causes major and terrible effects on people, families, and society. These effects can be seen in all areas of life, including physical and mental harm and long-term social and economic problems.

First, war can cause serious physical injuries, disabilities, and death to people. Using weapons such as explosives, guns, and chemicals can hurt people very badly. It can cause many people to die or get hurt really badly. They may even lose body parts or have long-lasting injuries. The pain that people feel from these physical injuries can be very strong and last a long time.

Furthermore, war causes great psychological harm to people. Constantly being around violence, feeling scared, and experiencing loss can cause a condition called post-traumatic stress disorder (PTSD), anxiety, sadness, and other mental health problems. War can be really hard on people's mental health, including both the soldiers fighting and the regular people who see or go through the terrible things that happen during war. These emotional hurts can last for a long time, which can affect a person's overall happiness and ability to live in society.

War also causes problems and breaks up families. During fights, families get split up because people have to leave their homes or join the military. This separation makes people really sad and unstable. When people lose their loved ones, either because they passed away or had to leave, it can deeply hurt their families. This can result in the breakdown of relationships and the support that they used to have. Children, who are especially at risk, often suffer the most from the consequences. They may have their education interrupted, be forced to leave their homes, and lose the care of their parents.

Furthermore, the effect of war goes beyond just the people and families directly involved in it. Wars cause problems for societies. This includes during the fighting and after it is over. When buildings like schools, hospitals, and important services get destroyed, it makes it harder for development and progress to happen. Money that could have been used for education, healthcare, and social welfare programs is being used for war instead. The movement of people and the problems it causes for nearby countries can put a lot of pressure on their resources. This can then lead to worldwide humanitarian crises.

The consequences of war create long-lasting problems for society and the economy. Communities have the job of fixing buildings, helping people who have been through tough times, and bringing back those who had to leave their homes. Making peace and feeling better again can be difficult and might take a really long time, maybe even many years or decades. Additionally, the strong disagreements and negative feelings caused by war can result in continuous or later issues, continuing patterns of aggression and uncertainty.

In summary, war has a very harmful effect on people, families, and communities. It hurts the body, messes up the mind, makes people move away, and causes death. Families are split up, and communities have to work hard to put things back together after the damage. The effects of war last a long time and can be felt by many generations. It makes it difficult to make progress and develop in every aspect of life. It is very important to keep trying to find peaceful ways to solve problems and avoid fighting, so that we can reduce the terrible impact on people.

# ECONOMIC, SOCIAL AND PSYCHOLOGICAL CONSEQUENCES OF WAR

War has far-reaching results that expand past the war zone. It has significant impacts on different angles of society, counting the economy, social texture, and person mental well-being. Let's look at each of these results in detail:

**1. Economic results:** War can have destroying impacts on the economy of a country, both within the brief and long term. Firstly, it leads to the pulverization of physical framework such as buildings, streets, and production lines, coming about in noteworthy money related misfortunes. The fetched of modifying and remaking post-war can be galactic. Moreover, wars require critical money related assets, occupying stores absent from profitable speculations in instruction, healthcare, and framework improvement.

War moreover disturbs exchange and commerce, driving to a decay in sends out and imports. Exchange embargoes, sanctions, and disturbed supply chains encourage compound financial challenges. These components collectively contribute to unemployment, destitution, and decreased living benchmarks for the influenced populace. The financial results of war can hold on long after the struggle closes, making post-war recuperation a challenging and extended handle.

**2. Social results:** War seriously impacts the social texture of a society, frequently driving to uprooting, relocation, and the breakdown of communities. The misfortune of lives, division of families, and the devastation of homes and neighborhoods make a sense of fear, injury, and separation among the influenced populace. Uprooted people regularly confront challenges in getting to fundamental necessities such as nourishment, shield, and healthcare, driving to expanded powerlessness and enduring.

War can moreover produce ethnic, devout, or political divisions, forces social pressures and fueling struggle on different levels. The breakdown of believe and social cohesion may take a long time or indeed eras to repair. Also, the relocation and disturbance caused by war can strain have communities that get outcasts or inside uprooted people, driving to asset shortage and social pressures.

**3. Psychological results:** War incurs extreme mental injury on people, affecting their mental wellbeing and well-being. The seeing or encountering of viciousness, misfortune of cherished ones, and presentation to extraordinary stretch can lead to post-traumatic push clutter (PTSD), uneasiness clutters, discouragement, and other mental wellbeing clutters. These mental results can endure long after the war closes, influencing people, families, and communities.

Moreover, the delayed presentation to savagery and uncertainty can normalize animosity and sustain cycles of viciousness in post-war social orders. Children developing up in war-affected zones may display indications of trauma and are at the next chance of formative issues and mental disarranges. The mental results of war amplify past people to society as a entire, hampering endeavors to revamp believe and set up enduring peace.

# CHAPTER 3: THE PURSUIT OF PEACE

## HISTORICAL EXAMPLES OF SUCCESSFUL PEACE NEGOTIATIONS AND CONFLICT RESOLUTIONS

There have been various memorable illustrations of fruitful peace arrangements and struggle resolutions all through the world. These occasions highlight the control of strategy, intervention, and compromise in settling debate and anticipating assist heightening of savagery. Here are a couple of critical cases:

**1. Camp David Agrees (1978):** The Camp David Concurs were a critical breakthrough within the Israeli-Palestinian struggle. Beneath the intervention of U.S. President Jimmy Carter, Israeli Prime Serve Menachem Start and Egyptian President Anwar Sadat come to an assention that driven to a peace settlement between their individual countries. This memorable agreement built up a system for peace, counting the return of possessed domains and the acknowledgment of Israel's authenticity by Egypt.

**2. Great Friday Understanding (1998):** The Great Friday Assention played a urgent part in finishing the decades-long struggle in Northern Ireland. It brought together different political parties and partners to arrange a power-sharing course of action and address the disagreeable issue of Irish reunification. This assention encouraged considerable changes, demilitarization, and the foundation of the Northern Ireland Get together, guaranteeing an comprehensive and quiet political prepare.

**3. Dayton Assention (1995):** The Dayton Assention finished the Bosnian War, which tore separated the previous Yugoslavia. Arranged in Dayton, Ohio, it set up a complex framework of administration and power-sharing between Bosniaks, Croats, and Serbs. This assention driven to the creation of the multinational peacekeeping drive and cleared the way for solidness and compromise within the locale.

**4. Oslo Concurs (1993):** The Oslo Agrees spoken to a breakthrough within the Israeli-Palestinian peace prepare. Beneath the intercession of Norwegian negotiators, this assention sketched out a system for interim self-governance within the Palestinian regions, clearing the way for transactions on a changeless arrangement to the strife. Whereas the complete usage of the Oslo Concurs confronted challenges, it illustrated the potential for tranquil coexistence and exchange between Israelis and Palestinians.

**5. South Africa's Move to Majority rule government (1994):** South Africa's serene move from apartheid to popular government offers a momentous illustration of struggle determination. Transactions between the African National Congress (ANC) and the apartheid government driven by President F.W. de Klerk come about in a tranquil settlement. This handle, guided by figures like Nelson Mandela, included compromise endeavors, a truth and compromise commission, and comprehensive decisions.

It secured a serene move and the destroying of institutionalized racial isolation.

These noteworthy cases illustrate that the determination of clashes regularly requires committed political endeavors, gifted arbiters, and the readiness of clashing parties to lock in in serene discourse. Whereas challenges and difficulties may happen, these victory stories outline that arrangements and compromise can clear the way for persevering peace and soundness

# THE ROLE OF DIPLOMACY, DIALOGUE AND NEGOTIATION IN ACHIEVING PEACE

Diplomacy, talking, and working things out are very important in bringing peace in conflicts between countries and within a country. These processes each have different things that help people talk, understand, and agree with each other.

Diplomacy is an important way to handle relationships between countries and solve problems without violence. This means using discussions and agreements between countries to resolve disagreements and reach solutions that both sides are happy with. Diplomats act as go-betweens, representing their countries' interests and talking to each other to create trust and encourage working together. By using peaceful methods, we can reduce long-lasting conflicts and find ways to solve any disagreements.

Having conversations is very important to create peace, whether the fights are between countries or within a single country. It means talking to each other in a nice way even if you disagree, trying to understand each other and find a compromise. Dialogue is a way for people who disagree with each other to talk about their problems and feelings in a safe and organized setting. It helps remove barriers, correct misunderstandings, and create understanding and compassion. Peacebuilding processes help to create an environment where people can talk and work together to solve conflicts and find long-lasting solutions.

Negotiation means when people who disagree try to find a solution that they are both okay with. This usually means that both parties talk and make compromises, figuring out what is most important to them and what they absolutely will not agree to. Negotiations can happen at different levels, like important talks between governments or just group discussions within a community. Experienced negotiators help the process by helping people find things they agree on and come up with creative solutions. Negotiations need you to be patient, flexible, and ready to find a middle ground with the other party, as you both strive to achieve a beneficial outcome.

Together, diplomacy, dialogue, and negotiation help solve problems and bring about peace. Diplomatic efforts help countries connect and dialogue allows for sharing thoughts and opinions. Negotiation helps people come to agreements by finding things they can agree on. These actions are not straightforward, but instead connected and constantly changing, needing ongoing dedication from everyone involved.

To achieve successful peacebuilding, it is important to use diplomacy, talk to each other, and negotiate to solve problems from their core, rebuild trust, and create solutions that include everyone and last for a long time. Throughout history, it has been proven that when conflicts are handled using these principles, there is a better chance of achieving lasting peace. It is important to remember that every conflict is different, and how we handle them should be adjusted to fit the situation, considering cultural, political, and historical factors.

# CHAPTER 4: ADDRESSING THE ROOT CAUSES OF CONFLICT

## UNDERLYING FACTORS THAT CONTRIBUTE TO CONFLICT AND WAR

There are various components that contribute to strife and war. These variables can change depending on the particular circumstances and setting, but here are a few common ones:

**1. Competition for assets:** Clashes frequently emerge from the competition for constrained assets such as arrive, water, minerals, or vitality sources. When assets ended up rare or unevenly disseminated, it can lead to pressures and clashes between bunches, countries, or locales.

**2. Ideological and devout contrasts:** Ideological and devout contrasts have verifiably been critical drivers of clashes. Clashing convictions, values, and belief systems can make divisions and fuel clashes as bunches look for to state their dominance or guard their standards.

**3. Power battles:** Control lopsided characteristics and battles for dominance can too lead to clashes and wars. When one bunch or country looks for to attest its dominance over others or pick up control over a particular domain, it can raise pressures and trigger clashes.

**4. Political insecurity and disappointments**: Political insecurity, powerless administration, and disappointments within the political framework can make an environment conducive to strife and war. When governments come up short to viably address social, financial, or political grievances, discontentment may develop, coming about in challenges, uprisings, or indeed respectful wars.

**5. Ethnic and tribal pressures:** Deep-rooted ethnic and tribal divisions can contribute to clashes and wars. Verifiable debate, personality legislative issues, and the crave for self-determination can worsen these pressures, driving to savagery and outfitted struggle.

**6. Outside impedances:** Clashes can be fueled or affected by outside on-screen characters. Obstructions by remote countries for vital, political, or financial reasons can drag out or raise existing clashes, as seen in intermediary wars or mediations.

**7. Financial components:** Financial aberrations and imbalances can contribute to clashes. Destitution and need of get to to essential assets and openings drive social turmoil and can give rich ground for the ejection of struggle.

**8. Verifiable grievances:** Long-standing verifiable grievances, counting uncertain regional debate or past clashes, can proceed to stew and contribute to continuous pressures. These grievances may reemerge and reignite clashes in case not tended to through strategy, compromise, or other implies.

It is vital to note that each struggle is one of a kind and may include a combination of a few variables. Furthermore, the flow of clashes can be complex and entwined, making it pivotal to consider the particular setting and subtleties when analyzing the causes of any specific struggle or war.

# DISCUSSING ISSUES SUCH AS INEQUALITY, RELIGIOUS TENSIONS, TERRITORIAL DISPUTES AND POLITICAL INSTABILITY

**1. Inequality:** Disparity alludes to the unequal conveyance of assets, openings, and benefits inside a society. It includes financial, social, and political abberations. Financial disparity can lead to destitution, restricted get to to instruction and healthcare, and need of essential necessities. Social imbalance can show as separation based on variables like race, sex, and age. Political imbalance can emerge from uneven representation and control conveyance among diverse bunches. Tending to imbalance requires arrangements that advance rise to openings, social equity, and comprehensive financial development.

**2. Religious pressures:** Devout pressures emerge when diverse devout convictions, hones, or philosophies lead to strife, separation, or the marginalization of certain devout bunches. These pressures can stem from chronicled grievances, competition for assets, or contrasting elucidations of devout writings. They can result in rough clashes, social avoidance, and encroachment upon devout flexibility. Advancing interfaith exchange, devout resistance, and regard for differing qualities are key to moderating devout pressures and cultivating tranquil coexistence.

**3. Regional disputes:** Regional debate happen when different nations or bunches claim possession or control over a specific geographic range. Such debate frequently emerge due to clashing chronicled accounts, competition for normal assets, key interface, or uncertain colonial legacies. Regional debate can lead to pressures, militarization, and indeed outfitted clashes. Settling this debate requires political arrangements, adherence to universal laws and settlements, and finding commonly worthy arrangements that consider the interface and rights of all parties included.

**4. Political insecurity:** Political flimsiness alludes to a state of instability or instability in a political framework, characterized by visit changes in authority, powerless administration, and a need of open believe. It can result from variables such as debasement, insufficient organization systems, destitute financial execution, social distress, or tip top control battles. Political insecurity undermines viable administration, hampers financial improvement, and can lead to social changes. To address political precariousness, fortifying majority rule educate, advancing straightforwardness and responsibility, and guaranteeing broad-based interest in decision-making are vital.

It is critical to note that these issues are complex and interwoven, frequently affecting one another. Viably tending to them requires a comprehensive and multifaceted approach that includes participation between governments, gracious society organizations, universal teach, and the dynamic support of citizens.

# CHAPTER 5: BUILDING SUSTAINABLE PEACE

## IMPORTANCE OF SUSTAINABLE PEACE BUILDING EFFORTS

Feasible tranquil building endeavors play a urgent part in guaranteeing the well-being and long-term soundness of social orders, districts, and countries. Here are a few key reasons why they are of most extreme significance:

**1. Conflict resolution and Prevention:** Maintainable quiet building endeavors address the root causes of clashes, work towards building and fortifying teach, and advance comprehensive and participatory decision-making forms. By tending to grievances, disparities, and socio-political pressures, these endeavors contribute to avoiding clashes from emerging or raising into savagery. In addition, they encourage successful determination of existing clashes through discourse, transaction, and intercession.

**2. Economic improvement:** Peace and soundness are pivotal for financial development and economical improvement. Maintainable quiet building endeavors not as it were build up a conducive environment for pulling in residential and remote speculations but moreover cultivate the improvement of framework, businesses, and markets. This, in turn, makes work openings, makes strides living benchmarks, and diminishes destitution rates, driving to more comprehensive and affluent social orders.

**3. Social inclusivity and cohesion:** Feasible tranquil building endeavors prioritize inclusivity, social cohesion, and regard for differing qualities. They point to bridge separates between ethnic, devout, or social bunches, advance social integration, and guarantee rise to get to to assets and openings for all individuals of society. By cultivating a sense of solidarity, resilience, and acknowledgment, these endeavors construct solid social bonds and decrease the hazard of social prohibition and radicalization.

**4. Environmental maintainability:** Feasible serene building endeavors moreover consider the environment as a imperative component of long-term soundness and security. They recognize the interaction between natural debasement, asset shortage, and clashes. By advancing economical hones, such as renewable vitality, capable asset administration, and climate strength, these endeavors diminish natural vulnerabilities, minimize competition over rare assets, and contribute to environmental conservation.

**5. Human rights and equity:** Economical quiet building endeavors emphasize the security and advancement of human rights, equity, and the run the show of law. They endeavor to set up responsible and straightforward teach, guarantee break even with get to to equity, and combat exemption for human rights mishandle. By cultivating a culture of regard for human respect, these endeavors make an empowering environment where people can unreservedly express their suppositions, appreciate their rights, and look for change for grievances.

In outline, economical serene building endeavors are significant for cultivating steady, comprehensive, and affluent social orders. They anticipate clashes, advance financial advancement, improve social cohesion, protect the environment, and secure human rights and equity. By contributing in and prioritizing these endeavors, we will make a more serene and feasible world for display and future generations.

# EVALUATING STRATEGIES SUCH AS DEMOBILIZATION, POST CONFLICT RECONTRUCTION AND TRANSITIONAL JUSTICE

**1. Demobilization:** Demilitarization alludes to the method of expelling or lessening weapons and equipped powers from a struggle zone. This strategy points to set up security and avoid the re-emergence of viciousness. It can be accomplished through different implies, counting deliberate yield of weapons, demobilization of combatants, and weapons devastation programs. Demobilization contributes to building believe, lessening the probability of assist viciousness, and making an environment conducive to peacebuilding endeavors.

**2. post-conflict reconstruction:** After a struggle, post-conflict recreation centers on modifying framework, teach, and communities that have been unfavorably influenced. This technique points to address the physical, social, and financial demolition caused by the strife, advancing steadiness and maintainable improvement. Post-conflict remaking includes exercises such as revamping harmed foundation, reestablishing fundamental administrations like healthcare and instruction, advancing financial recuperation, and giving help to uprooted populaces. It requires coordination among different partners, counting governments, universal organizations, and local communities.

**3. Transitional justice:** Transitional equity may be a comprehensive approach to address past human rights mishandle and advance compromise in social orders transitioning from struggle to peace. It looks for to address exemption, give change to casualties, and advance societal mending and compromise. Transitional equity instruments may incorporate truth commissions, tribunals, reparations programs, and regulation changes. These instruments point to recognize past wrongdoings, hold culprits responsible, bolster casualties, and cultivate a culture of regard for human rights. By tending to past grievances, transitional equity can offer assistance avoid the repeat of struggle.

It is critical to note that these methodologies are interconnected and complement each other. Demilitarization contributes to making a secure environment for post-conflict reproduction and transitional equity forms. Post-conflict recreation addresses the root causes of strife and makes a difference make the conditions for economical peace. Transitional equity guarantees responsibility, equity, and mending, which are fundamental for avoiding the reemergence of grievances that may lead to reestablished savagery.

These methodologies require facilitated endeavors from national governments, worldwide organizations, gracious society, and nearby communities. Also, the inclusion and strengthening of influenced communities are pivotal for the victory and maintainability of these methodologies, as they are the ones who will be specifically affected by the results of demilitarization, post-conflict reproduction, and transitional equity endeavors.

# CHAPTER 6: PROMOTING PEACE AT THE INTERNATIONAL LEVEL

## THE ROLE OF INT'L ORGANISATION, SUCH AS UNITED NATIONS, IN MEDIATING CONFLICT AND PROMOTING PEACE

Global organizations, such as the United Nations (UN), are important for resolving conflicts and encouraging peace all around the world. The UN was created in 1945 to make sure countries don't fight each other and to keep things safe and peaceful around the world. Let's learn about how international organizations, like the UN, help solve conflicts and promote peace.

International organizations play an important role in mediation. They help people who are fighting talk to each other and find a solution. Through talks and meetings, they help people who disagree with each other find things they can agree on, make deals, and come to peaceful agreements. Mediation efforts involve doing a lot of research, collecting important information, and having experts with technical knowledge.

Moreover, global groups allow people who disagree with each other to talk and negotiate in a civilized way. These groups provide places where people can meet, talk, and find solutions to their disagreements in a fair and unbiased setting. These platforms help people talk to each other, find middle ground, and find peaceful solutions to problems.

International organizations also help in keeping peace. When fights get really bad and people start using weapons, the United Nations sends peacekeepers to the places where the fighting is happening. Peacekeepers from different countries work together to keep things calm, shield ordinary people, and help make peace agreements happen. They make people feel safe, help provide help to people in need, and assist in rebuilding areas after a war or conflict.

Additionally, global organizations work on preventing conflicts by trying to deal with the underlying problems before they become serious disputes. They use different diplomatic methods, like talking, working out an agreement, and helping people come to an agreement, to calm down problems, make people feel comfortable with each other, and stop fights from happening.

Besides these direct actions, international organizations also support and promote human rights, help with development, and work on finding the main causes of conflicts. By promoting the growth of the economy, fairness among people, and safeguarding the rights of individuals, they strive to tackle the issues that frequently result in fights or disputes. These organizations help states by providing help, resources, and knowledge to build strong institutions and promote societies where everyone feels included.

However, we need to recognize that international organizations have some restrictions. How well they can solve conflicts depends on if the conflicting groups are willing to take part in peace talks and follow the agreements. Furthermore, limitations in politics, distribution of power, and disparities in countries' interests can affect their capability in reaching desired outcomes.

To summarize, groups like the UN are important for helping to resolve fights and encouraging peacefulness around the world. They help solve conflicts peacefully by using mediation, peacekeeping operations, preventive diplomacy, and addressing the main causes of the conflicts. Despite facing difficulties, these groups keep working hard to create a world that is peaceful and in agreement.

# ANALYSING MULTILATERAL EFFORTS AND THE IMPORTANCE OF GLOBAL COOPERATION

Working together with many countries and cooperating globally is very important in solving difficult global problems and making progress as a group. Multilateralism means that different countries or organizations work together to deal with shared problems, like climate change, international safety, human rights, trade, and public health.

Firstly, multilateralism promotes the idea of including everyone. It helps different countries with different views, needs, and resources to work together and find solutions they all agree on. When countries work together and share their resources and knowledge, multilateral efforts allow every country, no matter how big or wealthy they are, to have a say and contribute to making decisions that affect the whole world. This inclusivity makes sure that one country doesn't control everything, and that policies are based on what the whole world needs and wants.

Additionally, multilateralism helps maintain stability and peace by encouraging a global system that follows established rules and guidelines. Countries can work together and talk to each other through organizations like the United Nations, World Trade Organization, or regional groups like the European Union or African Union. This helps them solve problems and avoid getting into fights. These systems help people talk, solve problems, and work out disagreements, which makes conflicts less likely and helps make peace.

Thirdly, problems that affect the whole world are bigger than just one country and need everyone to work together to find the best answers. Problems like climate change, pandemics, terrorism, and migration require countries to work together and coordinate with one another. Working together with multiple parties helps us come up with plans, exchange information and ideas, gather support, and carry out actions together. If countries don't work together, they will have a hard time dealing with difficult problems on their own.

Furthermore, working together with many countries helps strengthen the governing of the world and the organizations that exist. By participating in group activities, countries promise to follow the rules, guidelines, and agreements made among nations. This helps make sure people are responsible, clear, and follow the same rules. Multilateral institutions also help solve problems, make sure rules are followed, and keep track of how things are going. When countries join forces, they can create and enhance rules and systems that help meet the changing needs and goals of people worldwide.

Lastly, when many countries work together, it helps make the economy strong and helps countries grow. Working together in trade, investment, and development assistance helps to make more opportunities to sell things, share technology, and improve skills. Countries can use their own strengths, work together, and share resources in areas like research, building things, and sustainable goals. This group effort helps things grow, makes things more equal, and makes people all around the world happier.

In short, it is important for many countries to work together and cooperate with each other to solve complicated problems, keep peace and stability, promote fairness in development, and follow international rules. Multilateralism means that countries join forces to solve global problems together. This approach promotes inclusivity, stability, working together, global governance, and economic prosperity. It recognizes that global issues cannot be solved by one country alone, but require a collective effort for the benefit of everyone.

# CHAPTER 7: PEACE EDUCATION AND CULTURAL UNDERSTANDING

## THE ROLE OF EDUCTAION AND CULTURAL EXCHANGE IN FOSTERING PEACE

Instruction and social trade play indispensably parts in cultivating peace on numerous levels, extending from person to worldwide. Their combined control lies in their capacity to advance understanding, sympathy, and common regard among individuals from different societies and foundations. In this comprehensive clarification, I will dive into the particular ways instruction and social trade contribute to peace-building.

**1. Promoting Cultural Understanding:** Instruction and social trade programs give openings for people to memorize almost diverse societies, conventions, values, and points of view. Through introduction to different viewpoints, generalizations and partialities can be challenged and debunked. As a result, people pick up a more profound understanding and appreciation for the abundance and differing qualities of human encounters. This understanding mitigates numbness, which regularly serves as a source of strife, and cultivates a sense of openness and acknowledgment towards others.

**2. Cultivating Sympathy and Resistance:** Instruction empowers people to create sympathy towards others by instructing them to see past them possess individual encounters and get it the challenges and triumphs of people from diverse social foundations. Social trade programs encourage upgrade compassion by encouraging coordinate intelligent between individuals from distinctive societies. Such intelligent make shared encounters and individual associations, breaking down obstructions and cultivating an appreciation for the common humankind shared by all.

**3. Overcoming Divisions and Building Bridges:** Instruction and social trade offer assistance construct bridges between communities and countries by encouraging discourse, collaboration, and understanding. By bringing together people with assorted foundations, these stages make openings for individuals to lock in in significant discussions, trade thoughts, and discover common ground. This common understanding and participation contribute to destroying misperceptions, generalizations, and inclinations that regularly lead to strife and threatening vibe.

**4. Supporting Worldwide Citizenship:** Instruction and social trade programs prepare people with the information, aptitudes, and states of mind essential to ended up compelling worldwide citizens. They advance basic considering, intercultural communication, and problem-solving abilities, empowering people to lock in helpfully in a globalized world. Through instruction, people learn around worldwide issues, counting social equity, human rights, and natural supportability, cultivating a sense of shared duty and a commitment to tranquil coexistence.

**5. Upgrading Discretion and Universal Relations:** Instruction and social trade play crucial parts in forming political endeavors and universal relations. As people ended up taught and uncovered to distinctive societies, they create the capacity to explore social contrasts and communicate viably over social boundaries. This social competence gets to be priceless in advancing tranquil transactions, settling clashes, and building positive connections between countries.

**6. Countering Radicalism and Radicalization:** Instruction and social trade programs serve as critical apparatuses in countering radicalism and radicalization. By giving people with information, basic considering abilities, and openings to lock in with assorted societies, these programs enable people to address radical philosophies and create a broader worldview. Education-based intercessions center on advancing values of peace, equity, and resistance, challenging the accounts that fuel strife and viciousness.

In conclusion, instruction and social trade are vital for cultivating peace. By advancing social understanding, compassion, resilience, and worldwide citizenship, these transformative devices contribute to building serene social orders and settling clashes. Grasping instruction and social trade as fundamentally components of peace-building endeavors can lead to a more agreeable and agreeable world.

# IMPORTANCE OF PROMOTING EMPATHY, TOLERANCE AND ESPECT FOR DIVERSITY

Advancing sympathy, resistance, and regard for differing qualities is of most extreme significance in today's interconnected and multicultural world. Here's why:

**1. Cultivating understanding:** Compassion permits us to put ourselves in another person's shoes, get it their sentiments, viewpoints, and encounters. By advancing sympathy, we develop a more profound understanding of distinctive societies, foundations, and worldviews. This understanding leads to exchange, participation, and eventually, serene coexistence.

**2. Building comprehensive communities:** Resistance and regard for differing qualities are the establishment for making comprehensive communities where all people feel esteemed and acknowledged. When we recognize and appreciate the special qualities and commitments of each individual, it upgrades social cohesion and empowers collaboration over different statistic lines. This, in turn, fortifies the texture of society and advances agreement.

**3. Breaking down generalizations and preferences:** Empowering compassion, resilience, and regard challenges generalizations and partialities that can sustain segregation and marginalization. By effectively advancing these values, ready to destroy hurtful inclinations and misguided judgments, cultivating a more comprehensive and impartial society.

**4. Sustaining individual development:** Sympathy, resilience, and regard are not fair vital for societal advance, but they too play a pivotal part in individual development. By grasping differing qualities, we extend our skylines, broaden our viewpoint, and create a wealthier understanding of the world. When we develop compassion, we ended up more compassionate and produce more profound associations with others, advancing passionate insights and in general well-being.

**5. Reinforcing worldwide citizenship:** In an progressively interconnected world, advancing sympathy, resilience, and regard for differing qualities is indispensably to creating dependable worldwide citizens. By grasping differing qualities inside and past our borders, ready to construct bridges, cultivate cross-cultural understanding, and work towards common objectives, such as tending to climate alter, destitution, and disparity.

# CHAPTER 8: OVERCOMING BARRIERS TO PEACE

## ANALYZING COMMON OBSTACLES AND CHALLENGES TO ACHIEVING AND MAINTAINING PEACE

**1. Conflict and Viciousness:** The foremost self-evident impediment to peace is the nearness of clashes and savagery, whether they are interstate or intrastate, ethnic or devout, or driven by political or financial components. The heightening of these clashes can make it troublesome to set up a feasible peace.

**2. Lack of Trust**: Believe is fundamental for any peace prepare to succeed, and the nonattendance of believe between clashing parties can make critical challenges. Deep-rooted ill will, authentic grievances, and a need of common understanding can all weaken believe and prevent advance toward peace.

**3. Political Divisions:** Inner divisions inside a nation or locale can weaken the peace prepare. Political competitions, control battles, and the nonappearance of comprehensive administration structures ruin participation and hazard re-igniting dangers. The need of agreement among key partners can make it challenging to execute fundamental changes and set up a enduring peace.

**4. Financial Variables:** Destitution, imbalance, and constrained get to to assets can fuel grievances and increment the probability of strife. In numerous cases, financial abberations are at the root of clashes, making it vital to address these basic issues for feasible peace.

**5. External Impedances:** Outside performing artists, such as neighboring nations or universal powers, can compound clashes by giving back to warring parties. Intermediary wars, arms deals, and geopolitical contentions can all complicate peace forms and amplify the length of clashes.

**6. Security and Demobilization:** Setting up and keeping up security is fundamental for peace. The nearness of outfitted bunches, expansion of weapons, and the challenge of demilitarization can posture noteworthy impediments. Guaranteeing the security of all people and reestablishing law and arrange are basic steps towards accomplishing and keeping up peace.

**7. Compromise and Equity:** Managing with the repercussions of a struggle includes tending to the grievances and injury experienced by people and communities. Accomplishing honest to goodness compromise and conveying equity to casualties can be a complex and sensitive handle, but it is vital for building economical peace.

**8. External Variables**: Normal fiascos, climate alter, and asset shortage can worsen pressures and contribute to clashes. In a few cases, natural variables can specifically or by implication disturb peacebuilding endeavors, requiring comprehensive approaches that consolidate maintainability and flexibility.

Overcoming these deterrents requires a comprehensive and coordinates approach, counting discretion, intervention, strife determination components, and long-term advancement activities. It is vital to address the root causes of clashes, advance discourse and trust-building, and guarantee comprehensive and participatory forms that include all partners. Economical peace requires a commitment from all parties included, as well as bolster from the universal community, to overcome these challenges and make a more tranquil world.

# STRATEGIES FOR OVERCOMING THESE BARRIES, SUCH AS PROMOTING DIALOGUE, FOSTERING TRUST AND ADDRESSING GRIEVANCES

Overcoming barriers in any circumstance requires a keen approach and the execution of successful procedures. When it comes to advancing discourse, cultivating believe, and tending to grievances, a few key methodologies can be utilized:

**1. Advance Dialogue:**

a. Make stages for open and important discussion: Build up gatherings, town-hall gatherings, or online stages to empower people or bunches to communicate and express their viewpoints.

b. Dynamic tuning in and compassion: Energize dynamic tuning in, where people endeavor to get it and regard each other's perspectives. Building sympathy makes a difference make a establishment for valuable exchange.

c. Lock in in valuable addressing: Energize people to inquire questions that advance more profound understanding and challenge suspicions, cultivating profitable discussions.

**2. Cultivate Believe:**

a. Construct straightforwardness: Set up straightforward forms and decision-making strategies to construct believe among all parties included. Straightforwardness makes a difference scatter question and guarantees responsibility.

b. Steady and fair communication: Frequently communicate upgrades, advance, and challenges, guaranteeing genuineness and unwavering quality in sharing data. Consistency makes a difference cultivate believe over time.

c. Illustrate unwavering quality and astuteness: Remain genuine to commitments and act with judgment to illustrate dependability. Believe is built through steady follow-through and moral behavior.

**3. Pay Keen Attention to Grievances:**

a. Make a secure and comprehensive environment: Cultivate an environment where people feel secure to specific their grievances without fear of repercussions or judgment. Emphasize inclusivity, guaranteeing all voices are listened.

b. Set up clear debate determination components: Create forms for tending to grievances, such as intervention, assertion, or formal request. Give people with a reasonable implies to look for determination and change.

c. Execute preventive measures: Proactively distinguish potential grievances and actualize measures to address them some time recently they raise. This may include worker preparing, strife determination programs, or approach advancements.

Keep in mind that these methodologies ought to be custom fitted to the specific setting and boundaries you're confronting. Adaptability, versatility, and progressing assessment of adequacy are fundamental. By promoting dialogue, cultivating believe, and tending to grievances, you'll be able make an environment conducive to collaboration, understanding, and positive change.

# CHAPTER 9: INDIVIDUAL AND COLLECTIVE RESPONSIBILITY

## IMPORTANCE OF INDIVIDUAL AND COLLECTIVE RESPONSIBILITY IN PROMOTING PEACE

Encouraging peace in our communities is something we all need to work together on, both on our own and as a group. Recognizing our personal role in contributing to peaceful living is the key to understanding why individual responsibility is important. Everyone needs to work on having empathy, being accepting of others, and respecting differences among people. This means being nice to others and respecting them, really listening to what others have to say, and solving problems without fighting or arguing. If we take responsibility for what we do and try to be better members of our communities, we can help make society more peaceful.

But, only having responsibility as an individual is not sufficient to obtain long-lasting peace. Governments, organizations, and communities all need to work together to make a peaceful environment. This means making rules that tackle the main reasons for fights, putting money into schools and programs that help society, and encouraging fair leadership. Moreover, it needs to encourage discussions and working together among countries, support peaceful solutions, and tackle unfairness that can cause tension in society.

By understanding that both individuals and groups are responsible, we can build a peaceful culture where everyone has a part to contribute. All person's actions and choices can impact others, which can eventually create a more peaceful and harmonious world. By working together, we can solve the root causes of conflict and strive for long-lasting peace that benefits everyone.

# WAYS INDIVIDUALS CAN CONTRIBUTE TO PEACEBUILDING EFFORTS IN THEIR COMMUNITIES AND BEYOND

There are a few ways people can contribute to peacebuilding endeavors in their communities and past:

**1. Advance discourse and understanding:** Lock in in open and aware discussions with individuals from distinctive foundations, societies, and points of view. By effectively tuning in and looking for to get it others, we are able bridge isolates, diminish generalizations, and cultivate sympathy.

**2. Hone non-violence:** Commit to settling clashes calmly and emphasize non-violence in our activities and intuitive. This incorporates dodging forceful dialect, advancing resilience, and looking for quiet resolutions to differences.

**3. Volunteer for peace organizations:** Get included with nearby peace organizations or community activities that aim to address social issues and advance tranquil coexistence. This may incorporate volunteering your time, abilities, or assets to back activities centered on struggle determination, intercession, or community improvement.

**4. Advocate for quiet approaches:** Remain educated almost nearby and worldwide issues and utilize your voice to advocate for arrangements that advance peace, equity, and correspondence. This may incorporate composing to your chosen agents, partaking in quiet dissents or showings, or supporting organizations that work towards tranquil resolutions to clashes.

**5. Advance instruction and mindfulness:** Recognize the control of instruction as a implies to anticipate strife and advance peace. Bolster activities that give get to to quality instruction for all, counting programs that advance peace instruction and struggle determination aptitudes.

**6. Cultivate resistance and consideration:** Effectively challenge preference, separation, and generalizations in you possess life and inside your community. Empower inclusivity, regard for differing qualities, and break even with openings for all people, in any case of their foundation.

**7. Engage in compromise endeavors:** Bolster activities that point to mend the wounds of past clashes and cultivate compromise among communities. This may include taking an interest in exchange sessions, truth and compromise commissions, or supporting activities that advance pardoning, mending, and understanding.

**8. Be a capable buyer:** Consider the effect of your utilization choices on peace and strife. Back morally sourced and created items, boycott companies engaged in conflict-related exercises, and advocate for mindful trade hones.

Keep in mind, it is through collective endeavors and the total effect of individual activities that we are able genuinely contribute to peacebuilding endeavors in our communities and past. Each individual incorporates a one-of-a-kind part to play, and together able to make a more tranquil and agreeable world.

# CHAPTER 10: CONCLUSION

## SUMMARY OF KEY POINTS

The book Tittle "Let There Be Peace" is all about saying no to war when trying to solve disagreements. The text focuses on important ideas mentioned multiple times

First, the book shows that war only makes violence and suffering continue. It helps to make people dislike each other more and keeps conflicts going. This says that using peaceful ways, like talking and discussing, is really important for finding solutions that will last a long time.

Secondly, "Let There Be Peace" talks about how war usually causes great harm to people's lives, families, and communities. This shows the very bad results of wars, such as people dying, having to leave their homes, and things getting ruined. The book suggests that we should use peaceful ways to solve problems and focus on making sure people are healthy and society is stable.

Thirdly, the book explores the harmful impact of war on people's mental health and society as a whole. This text looks at the emotional pain that people go through in conflicts, and how it can harm society in the long run. This text says that trying to create peace and using nonviolent methods can be helpful in helping people heal and creating a society that works well together.

Moreover, the phrase "Let There Be Peace" suggests that solving conflicts using peaceful methods requires individuals to have compassion, knowledge, and a willingness to consider different perspectives. This focuses on how important it is to create a peaceful and accepting culture to stop violence and encourage long-lasting peace.

In simple terms, the book "Let There Be Peace" argues against using war to solve problems and suggests alternative ways to deal with conflicts. This text talks about how armed conflicts can cause a lot of harm and suggests finding peaceful ways to stop them and create long-lasting peace.

## REITERATING THE SIGNIFICANCE OF WORKING TOWARDS PEACE AND REJECTING WAR AS A MEANS OF RESOLVING CONFLICTS

Striving for peace and saying no to war to solve problems is really important for many reasons.

Firstly, when there is peace, it helps create a stable and prosperous society. If there is no war, communities can use their money and efforts to make things better. They can focus on making schools, hospitals, and businesses. This will make life better for the people who live there. When problems are solved without fighting, people can focus on making things better for everyone and creating a more fair and happy society.

Peace helps countries to work together and have good relationships with each other. Countries can talk to each other and work together to find peaceful solutions. They can discuss and make agreements on things like trade, protecting the environment, and treating people fairly. This helps create a feeling of trust and understanding, which is the basis for working together towards common goals.

Furthermore, when we strive for peace, we are also supporting the safeguarding and advancement of basic human rights. When there is a war, people experience a lot of pain, being forced to leave their homes, and losing a lot of things. By making peace a priority, we show respect for the worth and rights of every person, no matter where they come from or their background. This helps create rules that protect people's rights, promote fairness, and stop more violence and unfairness.

In addition, it is cheaper to solve problems without fighting than to go to war. War causes a lot of money to be spent, which could have been used for making society better and building things like roads and buildings. By supporting efforts to build peace, countries can use their resources to promote long-lasting economic development, reduce poverty, and create strong and durable institutions. This, in turn, will lead to more stability and prosperity in the long run.

Lastly, it is important to select peace instead of war in order to safeguard the environment and deal with global problems. Wars can cause a lot of damage to nature, like making ecosystems very sick, ruining clean water, and adding to climate change by using harmful weapons and making people leave their homes. By using peaceful ways to solve problems, we can focus on protecting the environment, managing resources in a way that can last, and reducing the impact of climate change, so that the Earth is safe for the next generations.

In short, it is very important to strive for peace and not choose war to solve problems. It helps make things steady and fair, people work together, everyone's rights are respected, the economy gets better, and we take care of the environment. By making peaceful solutions our top priority, we create a good environment for progress, fairness, and a better future for everyone.

# DEDUCTION

To sum up, the book "Let There Be Peace" strongly argues against using war to solve problems. In this book, the author helps us understand the bad effects of war and suggests different ways to promote peace

The author is saying that war causes a lot of damage, not just to buildings and things, but also to people's emotions, minds, and society. The book shows many examples and stories of how war can hurt people, families, and communities for a very long time. It shows how much innocent people suffer when they are trapped in a fight between two sides, and how it affects the future generation in a very bad way.

Also, "Let There Be Peace" talks about how war often continues a cycle of violence instead of solving conflicts for a long time. This means that when there is a war, it creates a desire for revenge. And this desire for revenge leads to more killing and unfriendliness. And this keeps happening over and over again, never stopping. The book tells readers to think about how using guns and fighting doesn't usually solve problems. Instead, it usually makes things worse by making people even more upset and separated.

Additionally, the writer thoroughly examines different methods to solve conflicts that focus on peaceful ways such as talking, negotiating, and avoiding violence. The book shows how talking and working together peacefully can help solve problems and create lasting peace. This text suggests that we should support diplomacy and make international organizations stronger. This will help prevent and solve conflicts before they become violent.

"Let There Be Peace" also explores why conflicts happen and emphasizes the need to solve problems that fuel anger and inequality. This states that war doesn't usually solve the main problems and instead keeps unfair and oppressive systems going.

The book suggests that in order to create peace, we should take a comprehensive and inclusive approach. This means we need to consider the underlying causes of conflict and work towards creating a fair and equal society.

The conclusion of the book agrees with many famous peace advocates and organizations around the world. It emphasizes the important and immediate need to change how we think as a group and make peaceful solutions a priority when dealing with conflicts. It reminds us that peace means more than just no war. It means everything being in harmony, fair, and everyone getting along.

In short, "Let There Be Peace" is a strong message that encourages everyone, including individuals, communities, and governments, to fully reject war as a solution to conflicts. This text is saying that it's important to consider different ways to build peace. It suggests that using diplomacy, having conversations, and solving the main problems are all important. This is a reminder that if we work towards a world without war, we can create a better and more peaceful future for future generations.

*HAPPY READING!*